T0071016

To Henry Ley

PRELUDE AND FUGUE IN C MINOR

I PRELUDE

R. VAUGHAN WILLIAMS

Allegro con fuoco (♩=120)

Manual

f

Gt. to 15th coupled to Full Swell (closed)
(16ft. on Great & Swell)

Pedal

f

legato

© Oxford University Press 1930

Printed in Great Britain

OXFORD UNIVERSITY PRESS, MUSIC DEPARTMENT, GREAT CLARENDON STREET, OXFORD OX2 6DP

The Moral Rights of the Composer have been asserted. Photocopying this copyright material is ILLEGAL.

The orchestral material (score and parts) is available on hire.

poco animando
open Sw.
a tempo
reduce
close Sw.
legato
Gt. to Princ. Sw. 16, 8, 4

add Full Sw.

Gt. to 15th (with 16ft.) coup. to Full Sw.

add Full Sw.

Gt. to 15th (with 16ft.) coup. to Full Sw.

open Sw.
a tempo
reduce close Sw.
legato
Ch.
mp Ch. 8, 4, 2, coup. to Sw. 16, 8, 4, 2 (no Reeds)
mp legato
Ch.
Gt. to Ped. off
Ch. to Ped. on

add full Sw.

open Sw.
Sw. open
close Sw.
Gt. to princ. coupled to full Sw.
Gt.
Gt.
Gt. to Ped.
Gt. to Ped on, Ch. to Ped. off.

ff
Gt. to 15th. (with 16ft.) coupled to full Sw.

Sept. 2nd 1921
Revised July 29th 1923 and March 6th 1930

II FUGUE

Allegro moderato ♩= 80
Manual
mf sempre legato
Gt. diap. with soft 16 & 4ft.
coupled to Sw. 8, 16, 4ft.
Pedal
mf
Gt. to Ped.

add to Gt.

add Full Sw.
Ossia
Reduce to
Gt. soft 8 & 4 ft. coupled to Sw. 16, 8, 4 ft.

open Sw.
close Sw.
mf
add Full Sw.
mf
poco f add to Gt.
mf
poco f

f add to Gt.
f
ff Gt. to 15th (with 16 ft.)
ff
legato
sempre ff
legato
legato
open Sw.
Sw. open
ff

Aug. 23rd 1921
Revised July 30th 1923 and March 6th 1930
OXFORD UNIVERSITY PRESS